INSPIRED INNER GENIUS

Alexander Hamilton

The group of men that worked to build America is called the "Founding Fathers." Alexander Hamilton is an important Founding Father, even though he grew up without a father of his own and in a place far away from America.

The Founding Fathers

Alexander Hamilton was born on an island called Nevis around 1755. His father left soon afterwards, and life became difficult for Alexander and his mother. They had very little money. Sadly, when Alexander was about eleven years old, he and his mother caught a terrible fever. Alexander lived, but his mother did not. Without any parents, Alexander became an orphan[1].

Alexander went to live with a cousin, but he realized as an orphan that he had to take care of himself. He decided the best way was to become highly educated, so he worked hard to learn and read everything that he could find.

His dedication to learning and reading made Alexander a great writer! When he was a young man, a dreadful[2] hurricane swept across the island. Alexander wrote a letter to describe the hurricane[3]. When people on the island saw how brilliant his writing was, they raised money to send him to America to go to college.

Alexander Hamilton arrived in New York City. When he got there, the United States wasn't a country yet. Instead, America was a group of thirteen colonies[4] and the British king was in charge of them. Many people in America were upset with the British king and his country for treating them unfairly.

Even though Alexander was new to America, he dreamed that it could be a great country. He decided to support his new American countrymen to fight for their freedom from Britain. This became a war for independence[5] called the American Revolution.

At the beginning of the Revolutionary War, General George Washington met Alexander Hamilton. Washington was impressed[6] with Alexander's intelligence and courage, so he gave Alexander the job as his military assistant. Alexander worked hard for General Washington, but he wanted to fight in the war.

Finally, Alexander got the chance to fight at the Battle of Yorktown. Soon afterwards, the American colonies won the war and their independence from Britain. The people were happy to be free, but Alexander and the other Founding Fathers knew, without the British, that America was like an orphan too.

Of course, a country doesn't really have a mother and father. Instead, a country has leaders and important rules, called laws, for everyone to follow. Since America was a new country, it needed a leader and lots of laws to protect the people and keep them free. Alexander decided to help his new country by writing about important laws!

Article. V
Article. VI

It took a long time for the Founding Fathers to agree on a group of laws to be fair to everyone. With Alexander Hamilton's help, they finally created a list of laws called the Constitution[7]. This turned the American colonies into the United States of America.

The United States also needed a strong leader, which they decided to call the "president." The very first president chosen by the people was George Washington. President Washington gave Alexander Hamilton another important job of being in charge of the country's money!

Alexander made the smart decision to create a bank for the United States. This helped build a solid foundation[8] for America. To remind people of Alexander Hamilton's ideas and hard work for his country, his picture is on every American ten-dollar bill.

THE UNITED STATES OF AMERICA
1789
39922 A
FOUNDED A. D. MDCCXCV

Alexander Hamilton grew up without a father, but he became one of the Founding Fathers of the United States. He used his intelligence and courage to reach his dreams. To this day, Hamilton's dreams give Americans the freedom to make their dreams come true too!

GLOSSARY

1. orphan	A child whose parents have died or disappeared.
2. Dreadful	Something extremely bad or serious that can cause fear, unhappiness, or suffering.
3. Hurricane	A terrible storm with strong winds, typically in the carribbea
4. colonies	Areas that are settled and governed by a distant country.

Independence Freedom from outside control.

Impressed Feeling or showing admiration or respect for someone or something.

constitution A group of principles agreed upon by a nation for governing.

Foundation The action of establishing an institution or organization.

INSPIRED INNER GENIUS
Muse Museum

More IIG muses
to come...

Alexander Hamilton

1757 - 1804

Alexander Hamilton was born on the island of Nevis in either 1755 or 1757 (historians are unsure which year). Orphaned at the age of 12, Hamilton worked as a clerk in a general store and decided to educate himself for a better life.

Hamilton was sent to King's College (now known as Columbia University) in New York City. However, he didn't graduate because of the interruption of the Revolutionary War. Hamilton joined the Army to support the colonists in their fight for independence from Britain. He became General George Washington's aide de camp and eventually fought successfully during the Battle of Yorktown.

After the war, Hamilton worked tirelessly as a delegate from New York to get the U.S. Constitution passed by the Continental Congress of colony-states. As president, George Washington made Alexander Hamilton the nation's first Secretary of the Treasury, which allowed Hamilton to set up a national banking system for the United States that is still in use today.

Alexander Hamilton died from a gunshot wound inflicted by Aaron Burr during a duel of pistols in 1804. His portrait remains on the American ten-dollar bill, and he is the subject of the multiple award-winning Broadway musical production *Hamilton*.

Illustration of four of the United States Foundign Fathers, from left, John Adams, Robert Morris, Alexander Hamilton, and Thomas Jefferson, 1774.

INSPIRED INNER GENIUS

WHERE GENIUSES CLASH

Here at Inspired Inner Genius, we believe that every child is born a genius.
Join us in our journey to inspire the world, one child at a time.

Photographic acknowledgement (page 33) Illustration of four of the United States Founding Fathers, from left, John Adams (1735 - 1826), Robert Morris (1734 - 1806), Alexander Hamilton (1757 - 1804), and Thomas Jefferson (1743 - 1826), 1774. © Stock Montage via Getty Images

Cover designed by Irina Katsimon · Interior designed by Renata Christine ·
Written by Carrie Hollister · Published by Inspired Inner Genius

GRAB YOUR FREE EDUCATIONAL GUIDE!

This curated guide is the perfect educational tool to center a class around, to bring up at the dinner table, or even to spark an enriching conversation just before bedtime. Scan the QR code or visit us at **go.inspiredinnergenius.com/eg** to obtain yours!

CPSIA information can be obtained
at www.ICGtesting.com
Printed in the USA
LVHW050718050423
743358LV00003B/566